# History of Skateboarding:

## From the Backyard to the Big Time

### By Michael Martin

**Content Consultant:**
Pete Connelly
Staff writer, *Heckler* magazine

CAPSTONE
HIGH-INTEREST
BOOKS

an imprint of Capstone Press
Mankato, Minnesota

Capstone High-Interest Books are published by Capstone Press
151 Good Counsel Drive, P.O. Box 669, Mankato, Minnesota 56002
http://www.capstone-press.com

*Library of Congress Cataloging-in-Publication Data*
Martin, Michael, 1948-
   History of skateboarding : from the backyard to the big time/by
   Michael Martin.
   p. cm.—(Skateboarding)
   Includes bibliographical references and index.
   Summary: Describes the history of skateboarding, discussing the major events
and people of the sport.
   ISBN 0-7368-1071-4
   1. Skateboarding—History—Juvenile literature. [1. Skateboarding—History.]
I. Title. II. Series.
GV859.8 .M38 2002
796.22'09—dc21                                                    2001003920

**Editorial Credits**
Angela Kaelberer, editor; Timothy Halldin, cover and interior designer;
   Katy Kudela, photo researcher

**Photo Credits**
AP/Wide World Photos, 4, 10, 16, 19
Bettmann/CORBIS, 13
Capstone Press/Gary Sundermeyer, 20, 21 (all)
Jed Jacobsohn/ALLSPORT PHOTOGRAPHY, cover, 22
Patrick Batchelder, 9, 24, 29
SportsChrome-USA/Rob Tringali Jr., 6, 27; Lutz Bongarts, 14

1  2  3  4  5  6  07  06  05  04  03  02

# Table of Contents

Urethane wheels became popular in the 1970s.

# Growth of Skateboarding

In 1970, two skateboarders in Washington, D.C., tried an experiment. These skaters were Frank Nasworthy and Bill Harward. Nasworthy and Harward removed the clay wheels from their skateboards. They put on a different kind of wheel.

Earlier, Nasworthy and Harward had visited a company that made roller skate wheels. These wheels were made of a material called polyurethane. This material also is called urethane. Nasworthy asked if he could take some of the wheels home.

## Learn About

- Nasworthy's invention
- Beginning of the sport
- Popularity of skateboarding

Today, skateboarding competitions are shown on TV.

## The First Urethane Wheels

Nasworthy and Harward tried the wheels on the street. The new wheels were quieter than clay wheels. The ride was much smoother.

In 1971, Nasworthy and Harward moved to California. The next year, Nasworthy started a company called Cadillac Wheels. The company sold urethane wheels to skateboard companies.

At first, few people wanted to buy the new wheels. But most skaters changed their minds when they tried the wheels. Soon, all skateboards had urethane wheels. Nasworthy's idea had changed skateboarding forever.

## Popularity of Skateboarding

Skateboarding first became popular in the early 1960s. It has gone through many changes since then. Some people thought skateboarding was just a fad that would be popular for a short time.

Today, skateboarding is more popular than ever. More than 10 million skaters live in North America. Skaters are using new kinds of boards and inventing new tricks. Millions of people watch skateboarding competitions on TV.

# Skateboarding Slang

**1960s**
**hodad**—a new skateboarder
**hot dogging**—having fun by doing tricks

**1970s**
**bongo**—a bruise or injury caused by a fall
**gorilla grip**—a riding style in which the skater
  grabs the board edge with bare toes

**1980s**
**rad**—short for radical; used to describe good,
  fast skating
**thrasher**—a skater who knows how to
  ride well

**1990s**
**grommet**—a young skater
**shred**—to skate fast and hard
**stick**—skateboard

**2000s**
**sick**—great or good
**sketchy**—to nearly fall while performing a trick

In the 1960s, skaters were called "sidewalk surfers."

# The 1950s and 1960s

Skateboards were not sold in stores before the 1950s. People built their own skateboards. Often, they just nailed a board to a roller skate.

In 1959, California companies started making skateboards for sale in stores. Skaters stood on a wooden deck that had a rounded front end called a nose. The deck had a square rear called a tail. The deck was attached to metal roller skate wheels.

Surfing became popular in California at that time. Some surfers started skateboarding. Many people called skaters "sidewalk surfers."

## Learn About

- Sidewalk surfers
- Skateboarding bans
- Kicktails

## Makaha Skateboards

In 1963, California surfer and magazine publisher Larry Stevenson became interested in skateboarding. Stevenson designed the first professional skateboard. He started a company called Makaha Skateboards to make the boards.

Makaha started a professional skating team. The company also held the world's first skateboarding contest. This contest took place at Pier Avenue Junior High School in Hermosa, California. By 1965, skateboarding had become popular throughout North America.

## Safety Problems

The first boards had metal wheels. Later, skateboard companies used baked clay wheels. Both kinds of wheels were noisy and made the ride bumpy.

**Early skateboards were not safe.**

The skateboards were not safe. Skaters often fell when the wheels hit tiny stones. The boards sometimes slid out from under skaters as they tried to turn. Some boards even broke into pieces. Skaters did not wear helmets and pads as they do today. Many skaters had serious injuries such as broken bones.

**Skaters use the kicktail to perform tricks.**

## Trivia

Few skaters were interested in buying the first boards that had kicktails. Larry Stevenson had to run advertisements on the radio to sell these boards to skaters.

## Skateboarding Bans

People began to worry about the number of skateboarding injuries. More than 20 North American cities had banned skateboarding by the summer of 1965. In some cities, the police took boards away from skaters.

By 1966, few new skateboards were sold. Many people believed that skateboarding's time of popularity was finished.

Some people still believed that skateboarding could be a popular sport. One of these people was Larry Stevenson. He invented the kicktail in the late 1960s. This curved surface on the back of the board was a big improvement. It helped skaters control the board with their feet. It also made new tricks possible.

**Skating again became popular in the 1970s.**

# CHAPTER THREE

# The 1970s and 1980s

By 1970, few people still skated. But Frank Nasworthy's urethane wheels changed that fact. The wheels rolled over the pavement much smoother and faster than the clay wheels did. Urethane wheels also were easier to control. Urethane wheels were not the only improvement made in the 1970s. Companies made stronger skateboard trucks. This skateboard part attaches the wheels to the deck. The new trucks allowed skaters to make smoother turns. These improvements led to a comeback for the sport.

## Learn About

- First modern skatepark
- Invention of the ollie
- First skateboarding superstars

## Skateboarding Styles

Skateboarding's popularity spread east from California throughout North America. Millions of people began skating. Freestyle skaters performed tricks on flat surfaces such as parking lots and gym floors. Streetstyle skaters rode on obstacles such as city curbs and large concrete pipes.

In 1976, the first modern outdoor skatepark opened. This park was in Port Orange, Florida. Soon, hundreds of North American cities had skateparks.

Skateparks had wooden ramps. Many of these ramps were half-pipes. These large ramps are shaped like the letter "U." Half-pipes often are called vert ramps. The ramps helped create a new skating style called vert skating.

**Freestyle skaters perform tricks on flat surfaces.**

**Most tricks begin with an ollie.**

Matt Groening created the TV show *The Simpsons.* Frank Hirada was his neighbor when they were young. Hirada skated on his aunt's old car and ollied over fences. Groening never forgot Hirada's skateboard tricks. Bart Simpson later did the same tricks on *The Simpsons.*

## New Tricks

Vert skaters invented new tricks. In 1978, skater Alan Gelfand invented one that made him famous. He stepped down hard on his board's tail. This action made the board's nose pop up in the air. Gelfand's body lifted into the air and landed back on the board.

Gelfand's friends called him "Ollie." They called his trick an "ollie pop." Skaters later shortened this name to the ollie. Most of today's skating tricks begin with an ollie.

Vert skaters invented other tricks. Freestyle and street skaters started performing some of these tricks. More contests took place. Large crowds came to watch the skaters.

## Another Downturn

By the late 1970s, skateboarding again lost popularity. Many skaters still did not wear helmets and pads. The lack of protective gear led to many injuries. Many people believed that skateboarding was unsafe.

By 1978, hundreds of skateparks closed. Many were torn down or paved over.

## The 1980s

In the early 1980s, some skaters kept the sport going. They skated in empty swimming pools or on city streets.

A new group of skaters became well known. Vert skaters such as Tony Hawk became skating superstars. Rodney Mullen won most freestyle skateboard competitions. Street skaters such as Tommy Guerrero, Natas Kaupas, and Mark Gonzalez were doing ollies in the streets.

**Tony Hawk has been a top skater since the 1980s.**

**Skaters continued to compete during the 1990s.**

CHAPTER FOUR

# The 1990s and Today

The 1990s did not begin well for skateboarding. Much of the world was in a recession during the early 1990s. Many companies were affected by this slowdown in business. These companies included skateboarding companies. Some of these companies went out of business. But the sport did not disappear. Skaters continued to appear in videos and on TV.

## Learn About

- Early 1990s
- X Games
- World Cup Skateboarding

25

## Competitions

In 1995, the ESPN TV network started a new extreme sports competition. This competition was called the Extreme Games. Today, this competition is called the X Games. The tricks at the competition helped make skateboarding more popular than ever.

Skaters now can compete in street and vert events at a number of large competitions. Freestyle skating became less popular in the 1990s. Few competitions now include freestyle events.

Since 1994, the North American Skateboard Championships have taken place each May in Vancouver, British Columbia, Canada. This competition also is called the Slam City Jam.

In 1999, the NBC TV network began its own extreme sports competition. This competition is called the Gravity Games.

**The Gravity Games began in 1999.**

Most skateboarding competitions are part of a series called World Cup Skateboarding. This series includes events in both North America and Europe.

Skateboarding's popularity has changed many times since the late 1950s. But after 40 years, no one can say that the sport is just a fad. Most people believe that skateboarding is here to stay.

# Important Dates

**1965**—Many cities ban skateboarding because of injuries.

**1969**—Larry Stevenson invents the kicktail.

**1972**—Frank Nasworthy starts selling skateboards with urethane wheels.

**1976**—The world's first modern outdoor skatepark opens in Port Orange, Florida.

**1982**—The National Skateboard Association holds its first competition.

**1995**—ESPN begins the Extreme Games; this competition's name later is changed to the X Games.

**1999**—NBC–TV begins the Gravity Games.

# Words to Know

**freestyle** (FREE-stile)—a skating style usually performed on flat, paved surfaces

**polyurethane** (pah-lee-YUR-uh-thayn)—a hard, rubberlike plastic used to make skateboard wheels

**professional** (pruh-FESH-uh-nuhl)—a person who receives money for taking part in a sport

**streetstyle** (STREET-stile)—a skating style performed on objects found on city streets

**vert** (VURT)—a skating style performed on vertical ramps such as half-pipes

# To Learn More

**Burke, L. M.** *Skateboarding! Surf the Pavement.* The Extreme Sports Collection. New York: Rosen Publishing, 1999.

**Freimuth, Jeri.** *Extreme Skateboarding Moves.* Behind the Moves. Mankato, Minn.: Capstone High-Interest Books, 2001.

**Powell, Ben L.** *Extreme Sports Skateboarding.* Hauppage, N.Y.: Barron's, 1999.

# Useful Addresses

**International Association of Skateboard Companies**
P.O. Box 37
Santa Barbara, CA  93116

**Skatelab Museum and Skatepark**
4226 Valley Fair Street
Simi Valley, CA  93063

# Internet Sites

**EXPN.com**
http://expn.go.com

**Skateboard.com**
http://www.skateboard.com

**Skatelab Museum and Skatepark**
http://www.skatelab.com/museum.html

# Index